I0021968

Copyright © 2023 Empower You~ ~~~ ~~~

Printed in the United States of America
Published by: Writer's Publishing House
Prescott, Az 86301

Project Management and Book Launch by
Creative Artistic Excellence

iMARKET

Handbook

Optimization Guide

By Lizzy McNett

Stride Marketing Solutions

Table of Contents

30 Second Commercials

The 30 second commercial is a statement to describe the skills and services that your business offers. It is essentially a brief monologue that sells your professional abilities and reflects your ideal profile.

What makes for a good commercial?

The best business pitch depends on the message you're trying to convey.

In some cases, more concise ads are exactly what you need to hook potential clients and convince them of your value proposition from the beginning.

On the other hand, some commercials need a slow burn to establish a plot, ending in the reason consumers need your services.

No matter the length, the important part is that you take just the right amount of time needed to tell your brand story—no more, no less.

Studies Show

Studies completed by the World Advertising Research Center have shown that 30-second spots are ideal in order to effectively tap into all three components of a good brand-building commercial. It's enough time to make an emotional and intellectual connection, but not so much time that you lose the interest of the viewer.

30 seconds is the right amount of time to make a commercial that's creative, memorable, and engaging enough to entice the audience—which drives sales for any business.

The New York Times stated. "30 seconds are meant to have surprise value: they are usually over before listeners get bored -- leaving them interested in learning more information."

General Example:

- Introduce Yourself
- Solve a Problem
- Use Humor
- Identify an Issue
- Introduce Your Brand

Write a Good Biography

Can you choose three words to describe yourself?

Most of us have been asked this question, and many fumbled through it awkwardly.

Writing a personal description can seem daunting. However, there are times when it's essential - whether we're updating our social media profiles, blogging, or creating a website of our own.

Depending on the audience and goals, your bio can highlight personal interests, professional achievements, or a mix of both.

Here are some of the elements a bio might include:

- Job title or workplace
- University degree and other qualifications
- Hometown or city of residence
- Personal or professional goals
- Mission statement and values
- Skills and expertise
- Interests and hobbies

The goal of writing a bio provides people with a snapshot of who you are. There is a variety of reasons why you might need a bio, whether it's drawing people toward your website or promoting a blog, attracting clients and business partners to your brand, or highlighting achievements for job interviews.

How to Write a Short Bio

The most effective online bios are both professional and concise. Here's how to write a short bio that suits your business brand:

- Who are you? Introduce yourself
- State your company or brand name
- What services does your business provide the consumer? Explain your professional role
- Include professional achievements
- Why should they care? Discuss your passions and values
- Mention personal interests

Initial Paragraph

The first paragraph should tell the reader everything about you or your company. It should be no more than three sentences. Thereafter, it can be used on social media profiles or sites with limited character descriptions.

Spotlight Bio

Example:

Lizzy McNett, BA
CEO, Writer's Publishing House, Stride Marketing Solutions

An Expert in Developing Exceptional Processes to Brand Best-Selling Authors

Lizzy's Bio:
Literary Agent | Amazon International #1 Bestselling Author | Business/Marketing Speaker | 18 Years' Publishing Expert | BA, Fine Arts | Entrepreneur

Business/Personal Logos

Logos are symbols made up of text and images that help identify business/personal brands. They can bring added value. A good logo is the cornerstone of your brand. It helps customers understand what you do, who you are, and what you value.

Logo design is all about creating the perfect visual brand mark for a company. Depending on the type, a logo usually consists of a symbol or brand mark and a logotype, along with a tagline.

What does a logo do?

A logo makes you stand out from the competition. Perhaps the most integral part of a logo is giving your business a unique mark that differentiates it from other businesses.

Along with demarcating your business, a good logo also provides customers with some crucial information about the company: It can communicate the business industry, the service provided, target demographic, and brand values. A logo builds brand recognition.

Logos also leave a visual impact that reminds customers that you exist! In other words, logos can create strong visual associations with a business.

What are the elements of a logo?

While there is no definitive answer, there are some common logo design elements.

These elements work together to form different logo types.

Typography

Most logos will usually contain some kind of typographic element.

Color

Logos can be black and white, monochrome, or multicolored. Multicolored logos often have palettes that are either analogous, meaning colors of similar hue, or complementary, meaning colors of distant or opposite hue.

Context

In some instances, a logo is also defined by the context in which it is used.

Commonly we see logos online, on business cards, on storefronts, advertising, and in print.

Static or dynamic elements

When creating a logo, there are two options. One is creating a static logo that looks the same everywhere it exists, or a dynamic logo that changes depending on its context.

Logos are not the same as branding

Logos become a familiar icon that people recognize as the company name.
Consumers don't need to see the business name to know what the logo means.

Branding develops the image people have about what the company represents. It's how they serve the community, based on public relations.

Write a Great Tagline

A tagline is a short, memorable phrase used in marketing campaigns to convey the value of a brand or its products.

By definition from Websters Dictionary, it is "a pithy descriptor used in marketing campaigns to communicate the unique value proposition of a brand or its products. More broadly, the goal of a tagline is to leave consumers with a lasting positive impression of the brand."

Businesses use marketing campaigns when they launch new or improved products or services, break into new verticals or markets, and want to reinvent or differentiate themselves. The goal of these campaigns is to convey a promotional message to your target market and have the market act on it. Therefore, firms develop taglines to help accomplish this goal.

A tagline is designed to convey the value of the brand or products promoted in marketing campaigns. In other words, it encourages consumers to form a positive association with the brand in a short period. It boils down to a catchy and memorable phrase that provokes an emotional response about the overall brand. For example, the paper towel product Bounty uses the tagline, "The quicker picker-upper."

However, taglines don't always convey direct information about a product or the brand itself. Often, they describe a brand or product abstractly or merely appeal to customers on an emotional level.

Profile Pictures

As users scan through social media, thousands of profile pictures appear on the thread page. And every time you see someone's profile picture, you form an impression of that person. In a split second, you decide if they are likable, trustworthy, smart …or not. You judge them.

On social media, users are swiping right or left in their minds, connecting or dismissing, engaging with your content, or ignoring your connection request.

So, your profile picture is key to a personal brand and online networking. It will impact a job opportunity or ultimately business prospects.

Uploading a professional picture is a one-time action that provides lasting benefits. Therefore, it's imperative to invest some time in the best quality profile picture possible (no selfies).

Tips

- Show your face
- Frame your face
- Bring out the smiles
- Be comfortable
- Be unique but professional

What are Hashtags?

Remember the old days when symbols were something you used on a typewriter or dialed on a phone?

Now with social media and the invention of smartphones, it has brought about a whole new meaning to communication. Today when engaging on any social media platform, it's impossible to escape using some type of symbols like hashtags or emoticons.

It's not surprising that you may be unfamiliar with how to use, or the meaning of, a hashtag. It's a relatively new concept unless you're part of the younger generation. We all know how our children migrate to electronics.

Once we explain "what" a hashtag is, you will most likely know "how" to use them. At first glance, the use of hashtags might seem confusing. But it's a powerful marking tool to engage your audience with literally no cost.

The concept started because of the demanding competition within social media platforms. If you want to stand out from the crowd, the user must create a unique approach to having their post seen. Hence, the reason for hashtags and emoticons.

"The specific definition of the hashtag is a keyword or phrase preceded by the hash symbol (#), written within a post or

comment to highlight and facilitate a search"
WIXBlog.com.

The idea is that the post can be indexed by
the social network for anyone to locate even
if they are not one of your followers. By
increasing impressions, you essentially
improve marketing goals.

With the use of hashtags, your social
contacts are expanded to more than just
your followers. Think of this as content-
based marketing, similar to shopping on
Amazon where it shows you recommended
products in the same category as what you
have chosen. It has the potential of reaching
thousands of additional users, which could
lead to customers or new followers.

One concept that must be observed: It can be tempting to use a simple word like #write, but with millions of posts each day, the chances of it being noticed are small. A better option would be a more specific hashtag such as #lovewriting. It will allow you to follow specific hashtags and people with similar interests. Give the tag some thought before posting. For hints, use Best-hashtags.com.

Hashtags Have Three Categories

Content hashtags: As the title dictates, content hashtags pertain to your expertise, product, or service. They have the potential to greatly expand your brand.

Trending hashtags: A great way to capitalize on boosting your brand is using popular hashtags.

But use caution; remember to analyze the word ahead of time and ask, "Will this tag increase my brand, or get lost in the millions of other posts each day?"

The best trending hashtags are the ones that go viral: random moments about something funny, holidays, or spur-of-the-moment thoughts.

Brand-specific hashtags: If you choose to use a prevalent or generic hashtag, the posts may be lost in the shuffle. It's a good idea to create a unique word and be consistent. One great way to expand your brand is to get users to engage with incentives like discounts or free products. Plus, you can always test different hashtags to find out which ones get the best response, and no one is saying you must use only one hashtag.

One last word of caution: Do not go overboard. Using hashtags to write an entire caption can defeat your agenda. Each channel has a specific number of hashtags allowed in each post. The last suggestion is, only put hashtags next to a word with the most significance. Use the keyword of your post to choose the hashtag word.

Actions Tips:

1. Name
2. Business name
3. Author name
4. Book title

5. Product name
6. Special sale

Buidling Back Links

Social media is essential to having a strong marketing strategy. How you incorporate social media linking on platforms can either make or break the effectiveness of any campaign.

Social media linking can boost engagement, expand reach, improve search engine optimization (SEO), and enhance your brand's marketing efforts. Creating a clear linking strategy helps get the most out of social media marketing. It perfects the focus of the content you create and share.

The way you use links both on and off your site influences SEO. A great option is to establish a link-building strategy.

Link building creates more engagement on your website or external sites. These are also known as backlinks. Google considers websites with a lot of quality sourced backlinks to be trustworthy and valuable.

Social media is a cost-effective tool that can help drive traffic to your site, boost brand awareness, and improve your SEO. Therefore, it's advisable to incorporate social media into your link-building campaigns. However, it's helpful to understand that each platform offers different features and options.

Understanding the individual platforms allows for better targeting to maximize your links' effectiveness.

Action Tips:

1. Use Shortened and Branded URLs to Boost Social Media Engagement
2. Cross-Link Your Social Media Profiles to Grow Your Audience
3. Add Deep Links to Your Website to Improve Rankings
4. Use High-Quality, Engaging Images Alongside Your Social Media Linking
5. Incorporate Links in Your Social Media Profile Bios as Calls to Action (CTAs)

On the internet, understand it's not what you link but how you link that matters. Clear marketing strategies promote successful results.

Best Practices for Internet Searches

Internet Searching: The ability to search for subjects on the web is an essential learning model that anyone using technology should be aware of and understand. It can make life in the digital world much easier.

First, it must be noted that Google and others are not mere search engines; rather, you should think of them as AI, a vast hive mind that consists of us all.

A search engine maintains the following processes in near real-time:

- Web crawling

- Indexing
- Searching

Web search engines get their information after crawling from site to site. The "spider" checks for the standard filename robots.txt addressed to it. The robots.txt file contains directives for search spiders, telling it which pages to crawl. After a specific number of pages are crawled, a certain amount of data is indexed.

The term indexing means associating words and other definable symbols found on web pages to their domain names and HTML. The associations are on the public database and made available for web search queries. A query can be a single word, multiple words, or a sentence. The index helps find information relating to the query.

Typically, when a user enters a query into a search engine it is a few keywords. The index already has the names of the sites containing the keywords, and these are instantly obtained. Generating web pages comes from search results. On the top search, result items are snippets showing the context of the keywords matched. Such as:

1. Use unique, specific terms

The number of web pages returned on a web search is amazing. As an example, type in 'blue dolphin.' This term is relatively specialized, but a Google search of this term returned 2,440,000 results! To reduce the number of pages returned, use unique terms that are specific to the subject you are researching.

2. Use the minus operator (-) to narrow the search

Can you count the number of times a search returned something completely unexpected? Terms with multiple meanings can return many unwanted results. For example, when searching for the insect caterpillar, references to the company Caterpillar, Inc. are displayed. Instead, use Caterpillar -Inc to exclude references to the company or Caterpillar-Inc -Cat to further **refine the search.**

3. Use quotation marks for exact phrases

Many times, remembering a phrase or part of a quotation can be frustrating when trying to get quality results, so using quotation marks around a phrase will return only those exact words in that order. It's one of the best ways to limit the pages returned.

Example: 'What is an epilogue'. Of course, you must have the phrase exactly correct.

4. Don't use common words and punctuation

In a search engine search request, some common terms are called 'stop words' and are usually ignored. Punctuation is also typically ignored, but there are exceptions.

Common words and punctuation marks should be used when searching for a specific phrase inside quotes. There are cases when common words are significant: for example, Raven or The Raven return entirely different results.

5. Capitalization

Most search engines ignore uppercase and lowercase, even within quotation marks. The following are all equivalent:

- technology
- Technology
- TECHNOLOGY
- "technology"
- "Technology"

6. Drop the suffixes

The best search habits are only using base words: for example, instead of birds or walked, try bird or walk. One exception would be for a website that focuses on the act of walking, enter the whole term in that case.

7. Maximize autocomplete

Another useful technique is the order in which you enter the search criteria. Plus, the use of autocomplete is extremely beneficial. Selecting the appropriate item as it appears in the dropdown will save time typing.

8. Customize your searches

There are a few lesser-known options that help minimize the results and reduce search time: for example, the plus (+) symbol. Stop words are typically ignored by the search engine, but the plus symbol tells the search engine to include those words in the result set, such as tall +and short will return results that include the word and.

The tilde symbol (~): Include a tilde in front of a word to return results that include synonyms. A search for ~CSS includes the synonym style and returns fashion-related style pages. Examples: ~HTML to get results for HTML with synonyms; ~HTML - HTML to get synonyms only for HTML.

The wildcard symbol (*): Google calls it the fill-in-the-blank. For example, amusement * will return pages with amusement and any other term(s) the search engine deems relevant. But it will not work for parts of words, so amusement p* is invalid.

The OR symbol (OR) or (|): Use this to get results with either of two terms. For example, happy joy will return pages with both happy and joy, while happy | joy will return pages with either happy or joy.

Numeric ranges: You can refine searches that use numeric terms by returning a specific range, but you must supply the unit of measurement. Examples: Windows XP 2003.2005, PC $700 $800.

Site search: Many websites have their site search feature when doing research. It's best to go directly to the source, and a site search is a great tool. For example, site: www.intel.com rapid storage technology.

Related sites: For example, related: www.youtube.com can be used to find sites similar to YouTube.

Advanced searches: Use the Advanced Search button by the search box on the Google start or results page to refine your search by date, country, amount, language, or other criteria.

9. Use browser history

Using this option is great when looking for something that has been recently searched. If you can remember the general date and time of the search, you can look through the browser history to find the web page. This is not possible if you change settings and delete browsing history when the page is closed.

What is Meta-Data?

Meta Data can be explained in a few ways:

- It is data that provides information about other data
- Metadata summarizes basic information about data, making finding and working with particular instances of data easier
- Metadata can be created manually to be more accurate, or automatically and contain additional basic information

In short, metadata is important. If we use analogies, we can think of metadata as references to data. Think about the last time you searched Google. The search started with the metadata to find what you wanted. It may have been with a word, phrase, meme, place name, slang, or something else. The possibilities for describing a query seem endless.

Examples of metadata

As an example, to the naked eye, a rose is just a rose. But to the more discerning "meta" eye, a rose is so much more. It's the total of its meta.

You might be surprised by the amount of metadata that goes into describing an image.

Metadata information stored:

- The make of the camera
- Lenses used
- Time at which the picture was taken
- Focal length
- GPS coordinates of the location
- Image resolution
- Color profiles

Image metadata gives technical insights that are helpful during image processing. Metadata also facilitates easy search, retrieval, and backups and hence helps increase productivity.

Another example of metadata in an mp3 audio file.

Key metadata information:

- Audio format
- Encoding
- Channels
- Bit rate
- Size
- Band
- Album release date

Data is nothing but the total of its metadata. It is what helps us create a complete picture of our data and understand it in its entirety.

Alternate Txt

Alt text (alternative text), also known as "alt attributes," "alt descriptions," or technically incorrectly as "alt tags," is used within an HTML code to describe the appearance and function of an image on a page.

Alt text uses:

- Adding alternative text to photos is first and foremost a principle of web accessibility. Visually impaired users using screen readers will be able to read an alt attribute to better understand an on-page image.

- Alt text will be displayed in place of an image if an image file cannot be loaded
- Alt text provides better image context/descriptions to search engine crawlers, helping them to index an image properly

The best format for alt text is sufficiently descriptive but doesn't contain any spammy attempts at keyword stuffing. If you can close your eyes, have someone read the alt text to you, and imagine a reasonably accurate version of the image, you're on the right track.

A few examples of alt text for a delicious-looking stack of blueberry pancakes:

- Pancake alt tag example

Okay: <img src="pancakes.png" alt="pancakes">

The alt text is "okay" but it's not descriptive. There's more to be said about this image.

Good: <img src="pancakes.png" alt="Stack of blueberry pancakes with powdered sugar">

Not recommended

<img src="pancakes.png" alt="">

or

<img src="pancakes.png" alt="pancake pancakes pan cake hotcakes hotcake breakfast food best breakfast top breakfasts breakfast recipes pancake recipe">

Neither of these examples is recommended. The first line of code doesn't contain any alt text at all (notice the quotes are empty), while the second example demonstrates keyword stuffing in alt text.

Alt text offers another opportunity to include target keywords. With on-page keyword usage still pulling weight as a search engine ranking factor, it's in your best interest to create alt text that both describes the image and, if possible, includes a keyword or keyword phrase you're targeting.

Keywords

Keywords are ideas and topics that define what the content is about. In terms of SEO, they're the words and phrases used in search engines, also called "search queries."

As a website owner or content creator, the keywords on your page must be relevant to what people are searching for, so they have a better chance of finding your content among the results.

Authors must be careful to include website content that includes what people search for to find books. Therefore, writing a paragraph pertaining to your book genre can be very helpful with search engines including your site in results. As an example, if you write westerns, someone might search for western book authors, or best western books. The added content must contain those keywords to improve SEO keyword optimization.

Paragraph Example, "The western novelist Anna Elizabeth Judd provides it all as if you are in the saddle along for the journey. Her rare western books bring the readers joy from nearly every genre they can appreciate. She exuberantly creates the image and sentiments of the west to life throughout the storyline."

Keywords are the linchpin between search results and content provided on the results. The goal is to rank higher on search engines and drive more organic traffic to your site. The search engine result pages (SERPs), and the keywords chosen will determine what kind of traffic you get.

As an example, if you own a golf shop, you might want to rank for "new clubs" — but if you're not careful, you might end up attracting traffic that's interested in finding a new place to dance after dark.

Using keywords on website pages

Keyword usage must be intertwined with the page copy. Creating compelling content is about providing value for real people, not just sending hints to our robot friends at Google.

Creators can start with a keyword and create a piece of content around that term, but if the content already exists, you must figure out how it matches those keywords.

Next, create what's known as a "content to keyword map." Creating this map can help you understand the impact of existing content and identify weak links or gaps that need filling.

As keywords define each page of the site, you can use them to organize content and formulate a strategy. The most basic way to start is a spreadsheet (your "content to keyword map") and identify primary keywords for each article.

Build your sheet to add keyword search volume, organic traffic, page authority, and any other metrics that are important to your business.

Ideally, each page on a site will target a unique primary keyword. Generally speaking, the homepage will target a very broad industry term, and then you create category pages, product pages, and articles. The content will create a niche target market that applies to the business.

Author Categories

The most important category for your book should be the first one chosen. If you had to choose one category, this should be it!

Be specific; research the most narrow, relevant-to-your-book category you can find.

What are BISAC codes?

BISAC codes are 9-character alphanumeric codes that tell book retailers, distributors, and librarians what categories and subcategories a book belongs to.

BISAC codes are sent to retailers as part of your book's metadata. They tell retailers your book's subject, reading level, and genre.

Improperly chosen categories will inhibit potential readers from finding the book.

Correctly categorizing means your book will appear in relevant searches on Amazon and other online databases.

The secondary codes are used online – they mean your book can be merchandised in different areas of an online store, or marketed to customers with these specific interests.

Browser Search Results

Imagine a customer visits Amazon and types a keyword search for WWII Fiction. The reader browses the list, looking to buy, but your novel doesn't appear in the search results.

Book results don't appear by accident. It's an effective promotional tool that many self-published authors don't use to their advantage, yet it's information that authors must provide when submitting a novel for publication.

The product details, if done correctly, can boost search results and sales by getting your novel in front of buyers. Best of all, it's free! However, some platforms such as Amazon, Ingram Spark, Lulu, and BookBaby offer a variety of options for metadata. Ingram Spark offers the most advanced choices for metadata.

SEO Optimization

SEO Optimization: It's all about the algorithms

Search Engine Optimization (SEO) is the process of improving a website or app's presence in organic (free) search results. SEO differs from paid search campaigns where a marketer must pay for placement in search results.

What is an SEO audit?

An SEO audit is a review of a website with the intent of improving the site's rankings in organic search results. The assessments are performed with specialized tools, or by an experienced SEO consultant.

Why audit a website or app?

There are several reasons to consider an audit, but the most common are:

a. Organic traffic has declined
b. A redesign of a website or app
c. Site migration
d. Consolidation
e. Rebranding, or other major technical, content, link-related events

Website content must stay updated to keep your site ranking high in search engine results, along with eliminating outdated keywords.

- If the website contains content duplication it may cause an over-indexation or erode page authority. This issue lowers search engine results.

- Any blocked or hidden content could cause indexation concerns. Users will be restricted from finding your website if search engines cannot find all the present content.

- If your website has slower load times, visitors find the issue frustrating and it signals search engines to assign a lower rank. It will lower organic SEO results and conversion rates.

- A website that is not secure (HTTPS) could risk your visitors' privacy and can trigger warnings in their browser.

It is becoming increasingly important to have a more secure site. The same concept applies to non-transactional sites, especially if competitors have HTTPS security protocols.

- Poor mobile sites can lead to unsatisfied visitors, increased bounce rates, and decreased keyword rankings based on Google's understanding of low user satisfaction.

- Broken links (links from your website to other websites), inbound links (links from other websites to yours), or internal links (links from one page of your site to another) may lower your site's trust and authority.

- Google Webmaster Guidelines not being followed may lead to the devaluation of the site, making it less visible to users.

SEO Audits

The best practices for an audit are once or twice a year; however, it can vary depending on the industry or content strategy. Some examples:

- Website content changes regularly
- Code changes frequently on your website
- Multiple individuals contribute to your site
- Your industry changes quickly online
- Your industry is highly competitive online

The best way to think of having an SEO audit is by getting an annual physical with your doctor, or a wellness exam. Results show potential problems on the existing site, solutions to solve the issues, along with recommendations to increase performance.

Benefits of an SEO Audit

- Identify technical problems to resolve site performance in search engine results, thereby improving organic searches.
- Identify content opportunities
- Digital health analytics
- Current backlink profile
- Improve the overall use of the website for users and search engines

- Elevate rankings related to keyword searches, and increase conversations through leads and online sales.
- Establish a passive income through marketing channels
- Learn how search engines are viewing the website

What SEO Audits Include

Performance audits can include the following depending on your situation:

- Domains
- Subdomains
- URLs
- Redirects
- 404 page
- Robots.txt
- Indexing issues

- Crawl issues
- Canonicalization issues
- Page load time
- Structured data recommendations
- HTML and XML sitemaps
- Navigation and file structure
- Template-specific recommendations
- Internal linking strategies
- External linking strategies
- Keywords
- Page titles and meta tags
- Content
- Duplicate content
- Thin pages
- Under-optimized pages
- Data feed optimization
- Conversions

- Analytics
- Webmaster accounts
- Local targeting
- Citation improvements
- Image optimization
- Mobile optimization
- International targeting
- Google News inclusion
- Digital assets
- Social media indicators
- Blog optimization
- Information architecture
- Usability concerns
- Coordination with ADA requirements
- Knowledge graph optimization

How are SEO Audits Received?

Once the initial audit is completed, the analytics will be evaluated by one of our experts and then a meeting will be planned to review the results. A strategy can be created to solve the issues.

Free SEO Audit Tools

- Google Search Console is consulted before any actions. The domains must be accepted.
- Google Analytics – Analytics are crucial to the SEO audit process. Data provides the ability to track Key Performance Indicators (KPIs) and measure the impact of the recommendations for the audit results. The data provided in Google

Analytics allows us to track specific KPIs and measure the impact of the recommendations contained in the SEO audit deliverables.

- Bing Webmaster Tools – Bing Webmaster Tools provide insights that are not contained in any of the Google tools.

- Chrome Developer Tools – These tools allow the user to see how crawlers and browsers interact with your site. Page speed is crucial to any SEO audit. Chrome Developer Tools reveal which page elements are slowing users down.

Paid SEO Audit Tools

The paid tools for an SEO audit are almost endless, but below are a few of the favorites.

- MOZ – Keyword Research
- STAT – Keyword Rank Tracking
- PitchBox – Outreach Prospecting, Campaign Management, and Reporting
- Spyfu – Keyword Research and Competitive Analysis
- Ahrefs – Backlink Analysis, Outreach Prospecting, and Competitive Analysis
- Content King – Content Performance Tracking and Monitoring
- Crawlers

- Screaming Frog – Website Crawling and Searching and Extracting Code
- Deep Crawl – Web-based Crawling of Large Websites
- Arguments for and Against SEO Audit Tools

SEO audit tools can eat up a budget with little to no results, or the user finds the analytics vague and complicated, so it's important to understand your current needs. Granted, the tools give wonderful tracking performance if you don't have a robust team to sort through the particulars; however, the cost may be a waste. The best results come from a well-planned strategy, and that comes from individuals. In some cases, the financial expense may bring forth unexpected results in the end.

SEO Marketing for Local Branding

In many businesses, there is one common struggle that is difficult to avoid: competitors. The goal must be to gain traction over other local retailers. Although, going against the larger companies with auto-generated local listings is challenging. Plus, years of playing the SEO game increases the difficulty.

One of the most demanding obstacles for many local businesses is how to stay up to date with Google's ever-evolving list of ranking factors; updates like the "Possum" can disrupt any strategy. The algorithm changes allow businesses outside city limits to compete for local spots if they service that area.

SEO Tips to Help Move the Needle for Local Market Branding

Claim Your Business Listings

Once you have claimed your business listing, it is time to claim any duplicate listings that develop over time. The listings can be claimed and then any duplicates can be removed. Finding the listings can seem daunting, but there are tools to assist in this process. Moz Local is one great option to locate all local listings.

The process is easy: First, enter the business name and zip code. Be specific on the business spelling, capitalization, abbreviations, etc. Select your business from the results and Moz will serve you the complete, incomplete, inconsistent, and duplicate listings tied to your business.

Add Location Pages to Your Website

To get the best results when search engines crawl your site for the best possible matches, it is important to have a specific landing page for each of your business locations. The address should include suite numbers and the exact physical location.

Improve NAP Consistency

What is NAP?

"The acronym NAP stands for Name, Address, Phone number, and it's critical for any business that wants to rank well in local organic search results" (Corona, 2018).

Search engines need to have accurate information on the business name, address, and phone number (NAP), and this information must be consistent everywhere.

The information must be specific, not just your name and address. For example, if the title includes LLC, Co., or Inc., add the acronyms. Be consistent with the information listed on the website.

The Moz local search tool allows much of the information to be updated. Start with the Google Business Listing.

Update Everything on Google My Business

Accurate information is imperative for everyday traffic across the internet, particularly for optimized SEO search engine results.

Log into your Google My Business (GMB) account and update any outdated information. It is very important to fill in as much information as possible. Be thorough.

The listing should be appealing:

- Logo
- Avatar/profile pic

- Interior photos
- Exterior photos
- Product photos

All images should be high-quality resolutions. You only get one chance at a first impression. Update the info for all business locations.

Obtain Reviews

One of the most important factors in allowing your business to grow is reviews. People want to read what others think of your services, products, or customer service. Good reviews pack a powerful punch; however, the reviews must be legitimate, so do not fake them. If customers receive quality service, writing a review will not be a problem.

The reviews not only help your business ranking but also increase search results. By expanding real estate on a web search, SEO results will improve. As your demand increases, so will your Google ranking.

Peer ranking is a highly social advantage. When users see a 5-star review, it tackles three major components at one time:

- Ranking
- Click-through rate (CTR)
- Conversion rate optimization (CRO)

Create Local Content

When you create content in the business niche it will make an impact on the local search ranking.

Google AdWords Keyword Planner

AdWords Keyword Planner is a great **FREE** tool when it comes to establishing your local SEO keywords. The research will offer keywords that have the highest search volume along with the lowest. Plus, it helps you find similar terms for local audiences.

Backlinks from Partners and Sponsorships

Create a list of businesses and organizations that you partner with or sponsor, and then contact them and ask that they add a link to their website. Make sure you reciprocate the offer.

Local Link Building

Gaining backlinks from high-domain authority websites will significantly impact your local presence. This is one area that cannot be stressed enough.

Utilize Social Media Platforms

Do not underestimate the usage of social media platforms. They are a powerful financial asset at your fingertips. Plus, it's free marketing. Google will crawl and pull search results from social platforms, such as Facebook | Gab profiles and reviews, your business's LinkedIn or YouTube | Rumble, and even Instagram accounts.

In the next section are some suggestions on optimizing for local SEO growth. According to SEO Press Expert, "The ways of how we search using search engines and the content delivered to us are always changing. But one thing for sure is that search engines are clearly on a mission to provide users with the most relevant results for their query, personalized based on their location, search history, and browsing behavior" (Shaw, 2019).

The following is a checklist you can follow to optimize local business-boosting organic traffic:

- Boost SEO by adding keywords to any website
- Include business contact information such as name, address, and phone number (NAP).

- Always encourage customers to leave quality reviews.
- Be prompt when responding to reviews, even if it is negative. You will not be able to please everyone all the time, but use the knowledge to improve your customer service.
- Upload at least ten quality photographs so users will recognize your business quickly.
- Stay active. Keep business profiles updated with the latest news.

In simple terms, it means the process of improving your site to increase its visibility when people search for products or services related to your business on Google, Bing, and other search engines. The better visibility your pages have in search results, the more likely you are to garner attention and attract prospective and existing customers to your business.

Blogs

Why Optimize Your Blog Posts for SEO?

By optimizing posts for SEO, you can improve search engine rankings and get more traffic to your blog.

Since search engines are often the largest source of website traffic, this can be valuable to your blog, online store, or small business website.

If you're simply publishing blog posts and not optimizing for WordPress SEO, then you're limiting the amount of organic traffic hitting the site each day.

Action Tips:

- Plan Your Content with Proper Keyword Research
- Find Semantic Keywords for Your Focus Keyword
- Write an Effective Blog Post Title
- Make Internal Linking a Habit
- Add Images and Videos to Your Blog Posts
- Add a Meta Description to Your Blog Post
- Make Your Articles Easy to Read
- Use Categories and Tags to Organize Content
- Make Your Blog Posts Comprehensive
- Optimize Older Blog Posts

Many beginners tend to forget about a blog post after it's published. But, in fact, you are not done optimizing the blog post after writing or publishing.

Tips after publishing a blog post:

- **Share it with readers** – Share your new and old content with readers and subscribers. To learn more, see our guide on how to share your blog posts with readers.

- **Add internal links** – Once you have published a post, you can go back to relevant old articles and add a link to your new blog post. This gives your new articles link juice while also allowing users to discover them more easily.

- **Track search rankings** – You have optimized a post for SEO, but how do

you keep track of its search rankings?
See our recommendations of the best
SEO rank tracker tools for keyword
tracking.

Social Media Platform Posting

Since the invention of the Internet, the ways people can make money have become limitless. One fantastic way to increase any income is through social media. In fact, it can be very lucrative. Below are some outlets for making money through social media:

1. Endorse affiliate products
2. Create and promote information products
3. Sell products and services

4. Use visual media to promote your craft
5. Offer coaching or consulting services
6. Join partner programs

We have only listed a few ways to generate extra income using social media, and there are many more options. The important thing to remember is the process may not be easy to get started and will take time to become financially beneficial, but be persistent and don't give up.

Public Relations

The public relations business has gotten a bad rap over the years because most people do not understand what it means or what the job entails. Public relations promote a client's product or services in a manner free of charge to unpaid audiences. The idea is to generate a public understanding of the business's skills and industry in which they work. Below are five things every public relations person should know:

1. Public relations are like storytelling
   a) Write and distribute press releases
   b) Write speeches

c) Write pitches (less formal than press releases) about a firm and send them directly to journalists

d) Create and execute special events designed for public outreach and media relations

e) Conduct market research on the firm or the firm's messaging

f) Expand business contacts via personal networking or attendance and sponsoring at events

g) Write and blog for the web (internal or external sites)

h) Create public relations crisis management strategies

    i) Design social media promotions and responses to negative opinions online

2. Public relations is different than advertising

3. Understand the nature of the news
   a) Create the story
   b) Follow a story

4. Social media cannot replace traditional media

5. It is possible to measure public relations

Media is Your Friend

Media is an essential part of marketing any business. If people do not know you exist, how can they become clients?

Below are 28 ways to help get media attention for your business:

1. Learn what media outlets are available and target the right audience.
2. Use email over phone solicitation
3. Engage the right people
4. Schedule regular postings, stories, and engagement
5. Become the expert
6. Always be reachable
7. Create a resource center for your business
8. Comment with followers
9. Take advantage of freebies
10. Plan special events in your local area and invite the media

11. Engage on social media platforms
12. Offer to review products that pertain to your business
13. Write a complete press release
14. Be a resource for clients or followers
15. Avoid buzzwords and tech jargon
16. Use bullet points and pitches
17. Don't overhype
18. Do something unique
19. Create research analytics
20. Give shout outs
21. Invite the media to your special events
22. Start a Blog
23. Create your media shortlist

24. Attend community events where the press may be present
25. Watch publications with smaller and more targeted readerships
26. Hold a fundraising drive
27. Carefully choose your backdrop
28. Learn from your experiences

Social Media Marketing Tools

- **MavSocial** is a scheduling tool for social media (my personal favorite).

- **Sensible** is a scheduling tool for social media.

- **Buffer** is a scheduling tool for social media.

- **Buzzsumo** is a research tool that tells you how your content is doing and who is spreading the word.

- **Missinglettr** helps you automate the process of creating social content by scraping your blog post content and creating a year's worth of social content for you. It makes nine individual posts dripped out to your social channels over a year.

- MeetEdgar is your handy automated content manager.

- Hootsuite handles multiple social media accounts, bringing them under one login into a single dashboard.

- Mention is an extremely comprehensive social listening tool.

- Sumo has a whole suite of useful traffic and social media tools that can help improve your marketing strategy.

- IFTTT means if this, then that. This tool lets you set up rules that make running your social media marketing empire much easier.

- **Zapier** is another tool that encourages automation and does share some similarities with IFTTT.

- **Bitly** is a link shortener, taking lengthy URLs and shrinking them into much smaller ones.

- **Sprout Social** provides engagement, publishing, analytics, and team collaboration tools.

- **Design Wizard** is another tool that's good for making visual content, with a reasonably simple and intuitive interface.

- **Socialbakers** enable brands to work smart on social media through artificial intelligence (AI) to understand audience behavior.

- **Post Planner** makes it easy for you to find and share content consistently to get predictable, considerable, and remarkable results on social media.

- **Sprinklr** is a four-in-one social media marketing platform that can help you with social engagement, social advocacy, customer care, and social advertising.
- **SocialFlow** allows you to schedule your posts when your target audience is active and engage in real-time.
- **Brand24** gives you insights into what people are saying online about your brand. This tool helps you track your competitors, too.
- **Tracx** is the only social listening tool that provides an all-in-one solution that captures the full conversation.

- **ShortStack** has positioned itself as the most powerful marketing platform for contests and giveaways.

Affordable Graphic Design Tools

- Canva: Creative platform for graphic designers
- Pic Monkey: Photo editing and design website
- Inkscape: A powerful vector graphics tool that's free and open-source
- Krita: Free software packed with advanced drawing aids and templates
- GIMP: An incredible tool for any designer who works with photos
- Blender: The ultimate free tool for graphic designers creating 3D content
- Easel.ly: Online web tool to create visual infographics

- Adobe Graphic Programs
  - Adobe Spark
  - Photoshop
  - Illustrator
  - InDesign
  - XD
  - Lightroom
  - Premier Rush
  - Fresco
  - Audition
  - Character Animator
  - InCopy
  - Dreamweaver
  - Dimension
  - 3D designers
- Envato
  - Stock Video
  - Video Templates

- Music
- Sound Effects
- Graphic Templates
- Graphics
- Presentation Templates
- Photos
- Fonts
- Web Templates
- Elementor – WordPress website add-on program
- Placeit – Mock-ups
- Smartmock-ups

What is CRM?

Customer relationship management (CRM) is a technology for managing your company's relationships and interactions with existing customers or potential clients.

The goal is simple: Improve business relationships to grow your business. A CRM system helps companies stay connected to customers, streamline processes, and improve profitability.

CRM is a tool that helps with contact management, sales management, agent productivity, and more. CRM tools are used to manage customer relationships across the entire customer lifecycle, spanning marketing, sales, digital commerce, and customer service interactions.

A CRM solution helps you focus on your organization's relationships with individual people — including customers, service users, colleagues, or suppliers — throughout the lifecycle, including finding new customers, winning their business, and providing support.

A CRM tool lets you store customer and prospect contact information, identify sales opportunities, record service issues, and manage marketing campaigns, all in one central location — and make information about every customer interaction available to anyone in the business.

By understanding your customers better, cross-selling and upselling opportunities become clear — giving you the chance to win new business from existing customers. This helps grow lasting, more profitable relationships with your customers.

Better visibility keeps customers happy with better service. Delighted customers are likely to become repeat customers, and often spend more — up to 33% more according to some studies.

Customer Service

The invention of the internet has allowed business owners and individuals to connect with people all over the world. However, in this process, one-on-one communication often takes a backseat.

Statistics have proven on multiple levels that exceptional customer service drives additional repeat sales.

According to Salesforce, "89% of consumers are more likely to make another purchase after a positive customer service experience."

One great way to maintain fantastic customer service is by using SendOutCards.com.

Why Use SendOutCards?

Any one individual who owns a service-related business will in most cases rely on repeat business. In this case, it is imperative to stay in touch with clients.

SendOutCards.com is a great tool to do just that. Once you complete the initial setup, the system will automatically run throughout the year.

Public Relations is how a company interacts with its customers, both in daily transactions and with problem-solving solutions when issues arise. It has a direct and meaningful impact on a company's profitability, as customer service teams serve as the front-line response to the client's needs for long-term retention.

Learn more:

sendoutcards.com/u/lizzymcnett

A good marketing campaign is based on educating potential customers. People do not want to be sold. The best option is to communicate through your knowledge and expertise in the field you practice. When a person understands a concept clearly, it is easy for them to make an informed decision.

Writer's Publishing House has developed an exceptional process; a marketing strategy grows out of a company's value proposition, by which the client's campaigns shine above the competition.

Author Bio

Lizzy CEO is of Stride Marketing Solutions has developed a marketing strategy process for businesses to grow from a company's value proposition. A solid marketing campaign must address consumer demands to attract customers based on business confidence.

One valuable outlet to improve ROI is through social media, which has proven to be one of the most cost-effective targeting campaign options available. However, not all platforms are a good fit for every author/business, which is why consumer research is so important.

Once the best platforms are chosen the next step is optimizing metadata, and creating quality content to build organic followers. A good marketing campaign is based on educating the potential customer. Lizzy understands people do not want to be sold. When a person understands a concept clearly, it is easy for them to make an informed decision.

If your marketing campaigns are not providing fruitful outcomes, the solution could come from a few simple adjustments. Learn more by evaluating your current strategy process to once again grow from the company's value proposition.

Writers Publishing House was founded on the idea that the focus must be on the client's success. Lizzy believes, "Everyone should profit from their passion."

If you want to know more about publishing/marketing a book, please visit writerspublishinghouse.com where you can contact her about starting your book project today.

Lizzy McNett, BA

CEO, Writers Publishing House, Stride Marketing Solutions

An Expert in Developing Exceptional Processes to Brand Businesses.

Bio:
Literary Agent | Amazon International #1Bestselling Author Publisher/Business Marketing/Graphic Designer | 18 Years' Publishing Expert | BA, Fine Arts | Entrepreneur

Other Books: lizzymcnett.com

- IAuthor – Social Media Marketing Guide
- Stride Marketing Solutions– Alternative Media Business/Marketing Guide
- The Power of Thought

www.ingramcontent.com/pod-product-compliance
Lightning Source LLC
Chambersburg PA
CBHW070841070326
40690CB00009B/1640